The Bumper Brontosaurus

The Bumper Brontosaurus

ROBERT McCRUM

illustrated by Izhar Cohen

faber and faber

First published in this edition in 1997
by Faber and Faber Limited
3 Queen Square London WC1N 3AU

Photoset by Avon Dataset Ltd, Warwickshire
Printed and bound in Great Britain by
Mackays of Chatham plc, Chatham, Kent

Robert McCrum is hereby identified as author of this
work in accordance with Section 77 of the Copyright,
Designs and Patents Act 1988

A CIP record for this book
is available from the British Library

ISBN 0-571-17690-9

2 4 6 8 10 9 7 5 3 1

for
my god-daughter Anna

Contents

The Brontosaurus Birthday Cake

Bobby was seven years old and his head was full of dinosaurs. He thought about nothing else when he got up in the morning. He imagined meeting pterodactyls on the way to school. He imagined playing with tyrannosauruses in break. And when he came home in the afternoon, his schoolbooks were covered with prehistoric skeletons.

Every night Bobby dreamed about brontosauruses. They were Bobby's favourite kind of dinosaur. He knew everything there was to be known about brontosauruses. He knew what they looked like and where they lived. He knew how big they were and what they liked to eat for dinner. Bobby had studied the life-size brontosaurus in the museum until he knew it like his best friend.

The day came for Bobby's birthday. There were pink and green and blue parcels spread out across the table. There was a new book about megasauruses from his aunt. There was a dinosaur jigsaw from his granny, and a wooden model of a plesiosaurus from his father. And then . . . the lights went out.

Suddenly everyone was singing 'Happy Birthday to you', and there was a cake with eight candles blazing away in front of him. And when Bobby saw that it was in the shape of a baby brontosaurus, he was over the moon with excitement.

Bobby took a deep breath, gave a great PUFF!!! and blew out the candles. The room went dark and his father said 'Well done,' switching on the light in his business-like way. 'Now you must cut the cake.'

Bobby looked at the brontosaurus birthday cake. It seemed a shame to spoil it.

'And you must make a wish,' said Bobby's mother, handing him the family carving knife.

Bobby laid it gently on the smooth icing. The long neck was a bit like the spout of a teapot. The tail was thin and spiky. The brontosaurus birthday cake was quite fat. Bobby gripped the knife firmly with both hands.

'Don't forget to wish,' said his father.

'Don't tell us,' said his mother. 'Keep it a secret.'

Bobby closed his eyes. He thought: *I wish this brontosaurus was real.*

And he started to cut the first slice.

But the knife only just broke the surface of the cake. Underneath, it was hard and scaly. Bobby

squeezed his eyes even tighter together and tried again. The knife was jumping up and down in his hands.

Then his mother screamed, and his father said: 'Good gracious!'

Bobby opened his eyes just in time to see a baby brontosaurus with a perfectly charming smile shake the icing off his back with a wag of his long green tail. Bobby and his family watched in astonishment.

'It's alive,' said his father and twitched his moustache with annoyance. 'I think we should call the police,' he said.

The brontosaurus scrambled off the plate onto Bobby's knee with surprising speed. He was quite light and, although he had a scaly skin, underneath he was soft and warm. Bobby put his arms round him. 'Thank you very much,' he said. 'He's mine and I shall look after him. I'm the prehistoric expert round here.'

The creature wagged his tail with gratitude and smiled up at Bobby with a toothy grin.

Bobby knew very well that brontosauruses have big appetites.

'If we don't find him something to eat,' he told the family, 'he won't last long.'

'And good riddance, if you ask me,' said his father crossly.

Bobby didn't take any notice and went into the kitchen. The brontosaurus scuttled behind him. He was about the size of a new-born puppy dog, and his paws made a scratchy sound on the floor. Bobby offered him an apple but the dinosaur turned up his nose. So Bobby tried cornflakes, then a carrot, then half a cucumber, a sausage, a lump of Cheddar cheese, an orange, a hardboiled egg, a piece of toast, some pink jelly, a chocolate éclair, and finally a dog biscuit.

The brontosaurus looked offended.

Then Bobby caught sight of the peanut butter, his favourite food, standing on the table. He put some peanut butter on a plate on the floor. The brontosaurus sniffed it cautiously and then guzzled the lot with a snort of happiness.

When the ex-birthday cake had finished the whole jar, Bobby spotted something new. The brontosaurus was now twice his original size and showed no signs of stopping. He hoped his father wouldn't notice this as well.

As it was Bobby's birthday he was allowed to

stay up late and watch television. The brontosaurus sat with him and watched the football with great enthusiasm. When it was time to go to bed, he was given a box and some straw in the yard outside. That night, Bobby dreamed real live brontosauruses.

In the morning, it was school again. Bobby ate his breakfast in a hurry and went to collect his new friend.

'You can't take that thing to school,' said his father. 'It's against the rules.'

'And I don't want it in the house,' said his mother. 'It will make a mess.'

So Bobby left the brontosaurus in the back yard for the day. On his way home from school, he did not forget to buy some more peanut butter. It was a very hot summer's day and Bobby also bought himself a can of Coca-Cola. Soon he was feeding the peanut butter to his companion. But the brontosaurus was looking eagerly at the Coca-Cola.

'Of course,' said Bobby. 'You're thirsty. Try some.'

The brontosaurus swallowed the Coca-Cola in three mouthfuls and looked eagerly about for more. When Bobby's sister Liz came home, also with Coca-Cola, it drank that as well.

'The brontosaurus is much bigger than he was yesterday,' said Liz.

'SSSSSSSSSHHHHHHHHH!!!!!!!!!' said Bobby.

But their father had overheard them. 'I knew we shouldn't have kept it,' he said with a grunt. 'I suppose you think I can afford to have a full grown mammoth in my house.'

'He's not a mammoth,' said Bobby, 'he's . . .'

'Well, they're all fossils to me,' said his father with a frown. 'And I don't like it; I don't like it at all.'

The next day the brontosaurus drank a bucket of Coca-Cola and ate six jars of peanut butter.

'I think we should call the police,' repeated Bobby's father. 'There's probably a law against keeping dinosaurs like this.'

'Perhaps he will stop growing,' suggested Bobby faintly.

But the brontosaurus grew and grew. His appetite was enormous. He drank Coca-Cola in litres and ate peanut butter in bucketfuls. One day he saw Bobby eating a hamburger and fell in love with those too.

The first time Bobby took the brontosaurus for a walk in the park, it caused a sensation. No one

could quite believe their eyes.

'Perhaps it's a film,' they said.

'Or an advertisement.'

'Or a new kind of toy.'

But Bobby was certain. 'It's a real one,' he said. 'A real live brontosaurus.'

Soon the brontosaurus was the talk of the neighbourhood. Everyone wanted to see the amazing celebrity. He was invited to street parties in his honour. He was filmed for television and featured in the newspapers. Every day, at school, Bobby's friends gave him all the peanut butter, hamburgers and Coca-Cola the brontosaurus could possibly need.

'You may have been a palaeolithic has-been,' said Bobby affectionately, 'but you're certainly the talk of the town.'

The brontosaurus gave a protozoic smile as if to say, 'well, what would you expect from a real live brontosaurus?'

Huge crowds began to gather in the local park to see the brontosaurus and his master playing football on the grass. The ice-cream men and gas-balloon sellers and fortune-tellers and fire-eaters and card-sharpers and evening newspapermen and street musicians and even the blind beggars from the big city came hurrying there every evening. The mayor was not pleased. The crowds trampled on the flowers in the park. Besides, the mayor wanted to make money out of the brontosaurus himself.

When Bobby had finished exercising his prehistoric pet, he would lead him through the twilit streets followed by a mass of curious spectators. Bobby's house was suddenly famous.

'I wish these people would go away,' said his mother. 'It's really getting ridiculous. There was a newspaper photographer hiding in the broom cupboard this morning.'

Just then there was the sound of a siren and a police car drew up outside.

'I told you all this dinosaur nonsense was against the law,' said Bobby's father, lighting his pipe with a grim face. 'Now there's going to be trouble.'

'Excuse me sir,' said the policeman. These people outside your house are causing a nuisance and an obstruction.'

'I'm sorry,' said Bobby's father, 'but there's nothing I can do about it.'

'We'll see about that,' replied the policeman. 'I understand from my enquiries,' he went on, taking out his notebook, 'that you have a Brontysawrus on the premises.'

'That's right,' said Bobby's mother who, unlike her husband, had become quite fond of the dinosaur.

'I would like to inspect the animal in question,' said the policeman, who was a friend of the Mayor's.

'You can't take him away,' Bobby protested.

'We'll see about that,' said the policeman with a stern look. 'Where is it?'

'In the garage,' said Bobby's father, who was not happy having to park his car in the street.

Everyone went across to the garage. The brontosaurus was sitting peacefully in the darkness eating his way through a pile of hamburgers.

'How he's grown,' said Bobby's mother with pride as she switched on the light.

The policeman took one look at the brontosaurus and went very white. Then he hurried outside and slammed the door.

'Th – th – th – that animal's ag – ag – ag – against the l – l – l – law,' he said, with chattering teeth.

'He's very tame,' explained Bobby with a smile. 'He started life as a birthday cake.'

'I don't care where he started,' said the policeman. 'It's where he's got to that worries me.' He looked sternly at Bobby. 'How much more growing has he got to do?'

Bobby knew everything there was to know about

prehistoric creatures. Quick as a flash, he replied, 'A fully grown brontosaurus is seven metres high and ten metres long and weighs about fifty policemen.'

'That settles it,' said the policeman. 'I'm calling in the zoo.'

So the brontosaurus was given a special cage in the local zoo. One of the first visitors was the Mayor, who looked very pleased. 'At last my town has got a tourist attraction all of its own,' he said. 'I'm going to make a lot of money out of you.'

And he was right. Crowds of children and their parents arrived every day. Each morning there were terrific queues to get in. The zookeeper, who was the Mayor's brother, built some special seats outside the brontosaurus's cage so that he could charge extra money.

The Mayor's cousin, who had a chain of hamburger stalls, sold special brontosaurus-style hot-dogs.

The Mayor's sister, who owned a boutique, sold special brontosaurus T-shirts.

The Mayor's uncle, who kept a nearby public house, renamed it The Brontosaurus Arms and sold brontosaurus cocktails.

Every day, after school, Bobby visited his pet in his cage to make sure he was happy. Every day he watched him eat his evening meal of hamburgers, peanut butter and Coca-Cola.

The brontosaurus was now seven metres tall and ten metres long, as Bobby had predicted. And when he stepped onto the zookeeper's scales he weighed exactly fifty policemen. His hide was perfectly green. His long neck stretched out in front of him like a giraffe's and his tail was so strong that Bobby could go for rides on it.

'To think,' said Bobby happily, 'that you were once just a birthday cake.' He looked at the brontosaurus. 'It's a dream come true, you know,' he said, cracking open another can of Coca-Cola.

But then he saw there were huge green tears in his friend's eyes, running down his long neck and falling splash-splash-splash onto the straw in his cage. The brontosaurus was crying.

'Why are you so unhappy?' he asked. 'You have all the Coca-Cola and hamburgers you could want. There is no shortage of peanut butter, I promise. You are famous, primeval old-timer. What more do you want?'

The brontosaurus looked at him with big wide eyes and pointed his neck towards the door of the cage.

Then Bobby realized. 'You want to be free,' he said. The brontosaurus waved his great green neck up and down in agreement and the little old lady who was trying to feed him cream cakes almost fainted.

Bobby went home with great sadness. 'I must talk to the Mayor,' he said to himself.

But the Mayor was very cross when he heard what Bobby had to say. 'Stuff and nonsense,' he said, in his pompous way. 'I've never heard anything like it. All the animals in the zoo are happy. You ask them.' He looked cunningly at Bobby. 'Besides, the brontosaurus is good for business. The brontosaurus brings a lot of money to this town.'

'But he's not happy,' said Bobby.

'We'll soon see about that,' said the Mayor. 'Come with me, boy.'

So Bobby and the Mayor set off in the Mayor's

official car for the zoo. But when they arrived there was a terrible fuss going on.

'OH! OH! OH!' the zookeeper was shouting. People were running about with ropes and ladders. 'What shall I do?' cried the zookeeper. 'What shall I – ?'

'What's the matter, Jimmy?' interrupted the Mayor.

'Haven't you heard?' said his brother, his eyes as wide as moons. 'The brontosaurus has ESCAPED!'

The Mayor went as pale as a ghost. 'ESCAPED!!!' he shouted. 'ESCAPED!!!!!' he bellowed. 'Well don't stand there,' he yelled at the zookeeper. 'Do something! Find it – OR WE ARE ALL RUINED!!!!'

Then everyone went mad. The police went zooming around in squad cars with their sirens going full blast. The fire brigade was called out and sprayed water in all directions. Special detectives put on prehistoric disguises and went out looking for the brontosaurus. An APPEAL FROM THE MAYOR was broadcast on the radio and television. And a REWARD of ONE THOUSAND POUNDS was offered to the first person who found the brontosaurus alive.

And everyone who had been making a lot of money out of the brontosaurus was very, very unhappy.

Only Bobby was pleased. 'At least my antediluvian friend is free,' he said to himself, 'wherever he is.'

Days passed. The brontosaurus was nowhere to be found. Some people said that he had fled abroad. Other people said that he was in hiding in the nearby forest, or in the city sewers. Others said he was dead.

The Mayor grew more and more frantic. No one went to the zoo any more. The hamburger salesman and all the other businesses near the zoo went bankrupt. The reward was increased to TWO THOUSAND POUNDS.

Secretly, Bobby and his friends were pleased. Everyone knew that the way the Mayor had made money out of the brontosaurus wasn't fair.

Weeks passed. The summer leaves began to turn brown and the evenings became chill and misty. Bobby was allowed to stay up for the football, but he always wished that the brontosaurus was there to watch television with him.

One night he was lying in bed listening to the rain pattering down outside when he heard a

knock at the window. He jumped up. There was the familiar face of the brontosaurus peering in through the window.

Bobby rushed downstairs to get the brontosaurus off the street before the police saw him. Soon, he was settling his runaway friend into the back garden and trying not to knock over his father's prize roses.

'Welcome home, errant fossil,' he said, affectionately patting the familiar green hide.

The dinosaur wagged his tail and nodded with enthusiasm, as if to say he was glad to see Bobby again.

But after that Bobby could hardly sleep for excitement and worry. What was he going to do with his massive pet? There was no way he could hide him in the garage or the garden. People would soon find out and try to claim the reward. How could he stop the brontosaurus being taken back to the Mayor's zoo?

Bobby lay awake with his puzzle and watched the stars move across the sky. Gradually an idea took shape in his mind.

It was still dark when he crept downstairs into the garden. PSSSTT!

But the brontosaurus was already awake, shivering in the cold.

Bobby could see at once that the dinosaur was unhappy. 'You can't stay here,' he said. 'You'll end up in the zoo. That Mayor's not to be trusted with a megalithic rarity.'

The brontosaurus made a noise like 'Brrgh', and nodded his head in agreement. 'So I'm going to tell the Mayor I've found you.'

The fugitive looked surprised.

'Don't worry. By the time he hears about this, you'll be miles away.' He looked knowingly at the brontosaurus. 'In the secret places you've been hiding all these weeks. I know all there is to know about you prehistoric types. Popping up in birthday cakes is not your only trick.'

The monster looked a bit sheepish, as if to say, well, you're right of course. Bobby placed a hand on the scaly shoulder. 'Besides,' he said, 'after the Ice Age you need a break.' He looked up at the sky. It was getting light. 'Now off you go.'

The brontosaurus looked at him sadly.

'I shall miss you too, but it's better this way. I'll always know where to find you.' Bobby smiled. 'Cheer up. The Mayor will never know where you are. And once I've told him that you've been discovered he will forget about the reward.'

The brontosaurus could see that all this made sense, and so, with a shake of his big green tail, he lumbered through the garden fence and disappeared into the dawn.

When they got up for breakfast, Bobby's mother and father were astonished to hear the news.

'You've found the brontosaurus!' they exclaimed.

'Where is it?' asked his father. 'I'm calling the police.'

'No you're not,' said Bobby firmly. 'Because he's not here. He's gone away again – and I'm the only one who knows where he is.'

'I don't believe you,' said his father sourly.

But when Bobby showed him the huge footprints in the rose garden, he realized it was true after all.

'And now I must go and see the Mayor,' said Bobby, and rushed off to the town hall.

'I'm sorry, young man,' said the town hall official (who was the Mayor's nephew), 'but the Mayor is in a council meeting.'

'But – but I've found the brontosaurus,' said Bobby.

The official looked at Bobby in astonishment. 'YOU'VE FOUND THE BRONTOSAURUS!!!!!' he gasped, and ran to find his uncle.

In a few moments the Mayor came hurrying out, surrounded by all his people, very excited. 'Well, well, well,' said the Mayor, patting Bobby on the head. 'So we've found the brontosaurus have we?'

'Yes,' said Bobby.

'Well, come on.' The Mayor was stern. 'Tell us where it is. I haven't got all day, you know.'

Bobby looked steadily at the Mayor. 'The brontosaurus doesn't like the way you do things round here. He's decided he will never come back.'

The Mayor and all the people from the town hall stared at each other in astonishment. 'Never come back!' they exclaimed.

'That's right,' said Bobby. 'I'm the only one who knows where he is.' He smiled. 'And I intend to keep it a secret.'

The Mayor looked very cross and pompous. 'You realize, young man, that you're waving goodbye to Two Thousand Pounds. I'd think again if I was you.'

'That's fine by me,' said Bobby simply. 'The brontosaurus stays free.'

The Mayor and all the people from the town hall

were very, very unhappy. But there was nothing they could do.

'Back to work, boys,' said the Mayor, who knew when he was beaten. 'I suppose all good things have to come to an end sometime,' he added in a small voice.

So Bobby went home to his family and told them what had happened at the town hall. His father seemed a bit unhappy about the Two Thousand Pounds, but his mother and his sister Liz were delighted that the Mayor had been outwitted at last.

Life wasn't quite the same as before, but at least they all knew that the brontosaurus was free and happy. And anyway there was really no knowing when he wouldn't burst back into their lives . . .

Brontosaurus Superstar

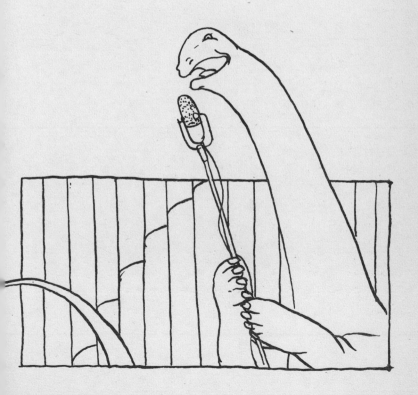

It was *his* brontosaurus. There could be no doubt of that. Bobby stared at the newspaper on the breakfast table.

MUSICAL MONSTER
WOWS THE WILD WEST!

'Look,' he said to his mother as she gave him his breakfast. 'My brontosaurus has become an American hit!'

'I always knew he had star quality,' she replied, calmly studying the photographs.

Full of excitement, Bobby took the newspaper to show his friends at school.

'The brontosaurus has always wanted to go to America,' he explained. 'They have all the hamburgers and Coca-Cola in the world. The television is on all day and all night. America's the best.'

'When will you go and see him?' they asked.

'Oh – ' Bobby looked important. 'I expect I'll get an invitation very soon.'

All his friends were very impressed.

The headmaster was also fond of Bobby's brontosaurus. Last year it had given away the prizes. Today, he read out the newspaper to the whole school.

'Hollywood,' he began, 'the home of the stars, has been swept away by brontosaurus-fever. The talk of the town is the new musical, *Bones!*, which has been breaking all box-office records. The singing and dancing lead in this prehistoric extravaganza is a fifty-ton brontosaurus which, to the amazement of the audiences, turns out to be a real one. The brontosaurus is, of course, the latest discovery of I. Samuel Gold, of Gold Studios, the world-famous impresario and producer.'

Bobby's friends looked at the newspaper.

'I bet you don't know what an impresario is,' he said.

'How do you know he's your brontosaurus?' they asked, ignoring his remark.

'My brontosaurus has always had star quality,' Bobby replied in a superior voice.

He had known for a long time that his Ice Age pet had an ambition to go on the stage. At their last meeting, the brontosaurus had given a demonstration of his disco-dancing.

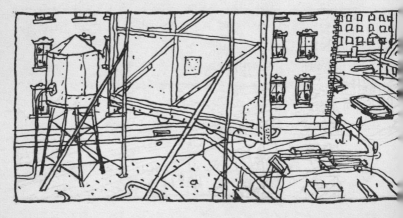

And now the primeval old-timer had made it big.

The rest of the day at school passed like a dream. Bobby was asked for his autograph. The local paper sent someone to take a picture. Even the wicked Mayor rang up to say how proud he was of the way the brontosaurus was putting his town on the map.

'So what are you going to do now?' asked Bobby's friends.

'Oh, I expect I shall go to Hollywood to manage his interests,' he said grandly.

But when he got home his father was very stern. 'You're staying at school, young man,' he said, puffing on his pipe. 'And you're getting a proper education. I'm not having you gallivanting off to Hollywood just because they're writing about the brontosaurus in the newspaper. Whoever believed what they say in the newspapers?' he added with a snort.

'If you don't let me go,' said Bobby, 'I shall run away.'

'That's enough of that,' said his mother. 'If the brontosaurus is your friend he will invite you to come and visit him. You wait and see.'

But the months passed and no invitation arrived. The brontosaurus became more and more famous. He was featured on the cover of *Time* and *Newsweek*. He was modelled for Madame Tussaud's. Everyone was talking about *Bones!* He was even photographed at weddings and nightclubs.

'No doubt about it,' said Bobby's headmaster. 'Your dinosaur is the flavour of the month.'

The time came for Bobby's birthday. He was going to be ten.

'How funny to think,' said his mother, 'only two years ago, the brontosaurus was just a birthday cake.'

'And here's another surprise for you,' said his father, smiling for the first time that year, as he handed his son an envelope.

'What's this?' asked Bobby.

'Open it and see.'

Inside there were four aeroplane tickets for Hollywood. 'We're going to see the brontosaurus after all,' said Bobby's mother (who was of course just as fond of the dinosaur as her son).

So there they were. In Hollywood. They walked around for a while, staring at all the amazing sights.

'I'm glad I don't live here,' said Bobby's mother. 'These hills would kill me.'

'I don't think much of a place that doesn't have a good cricket pitch,' said his father.

'So what do we do now?' asked his sister.

They were all standing next to a huge advertisement:

SEE BONES!
SEE THE SENSATIONAL BRONTOSAURUS!

'I think we should all get tickets for the show,' said Bobby. 'Then we can go to the stage door afterwards and find the brontosaurus.'

Bones! was being performed in the biggest theatre Bobby had ever seen, full of the smartest people he had ever seen. His father bought four tickets for the front row and they took their seats in great excitement. When the music started, the lights went down and – Wow!

Bobby gasped.

There – right in front of him, as large as life – was the brontosaurus. He was wearing a silver space suit and a golden helmet like an astronaut and he was descending slowly onto the stage on a huge model space rocket.

All at once the stage was full of singers and dancers in prehistoric costumes.

The show had begun.

Halfway through, during the interval, Bobby whispered to his sister Liz, 'I don't think the brontosaurus is much good, do you?'

And she shook her head in agreement.

After it was all over and the brontosaurus had made his last bow, they all went off to the stage door to find their scaly friend.

'You can't go in there,' said the doorman. 'That's where the brontosaurus has his dressing room.'

'But we're his oldest fans,' said Bobby.

'I've heard that one before,' said the doorman.

'This is my family,' protested Bobby. 'We've come all the way from England to see him again. You've got to let us in.'

'Orders is orders,' said the doorman. 'It's more than my job's worth.'

They were overheard by a short fat man with silver hair and gold buttons on his white suit.

'Hi, gang,' he interrupted. 'Who says you've got to see the brontosaurus?'

'Who are you?' demanded Bobby's father, who had made up his mind to hate America.

'My name,' said the fat man impressively, 'is

Samuel Gold. I. Samuel Gold of Gold Studios. I manage the brontosaurus.' He handed over his card. 'Listen, kid,' he said to Bobby, 'come to my office tomorrow and I'll give you an audition. You want my Money and Fame contract? No problem. With me, the dollars is automatic. When you're a star the sky's the limit.'

'I don't want an audition,' said Bobby. 'I want to say hello to my brontosaurus.'

'The brontosaurus talks to no one,' said I. Samuel Gold. He nodded to the doorman. 'Show them out, Herb.'

Suddenly, Bobby and his family found themselves in a deserted street outside the theatre.

'Where do we go from here?' asked Liz.

'Well,' said Bobby the next morning. 'It says in the newspapers that the brontosaurus has a house by the sea. Let's go and see if we can find him.'

So they hired a car the size of Tennessee and set off down the coast. It was a sunny day and the sea

was sparkling like diamonds.

'Once we find the brontosaurus at home,' they said to each other, 'this is going to be the best holiday we've ever had.'

They came round a corner and –

'There!' said Bobby.

The brontosaurus's villa was built on the edge of a cliff in the shape of an Ice Age cave.

'Fabulous,' said Liz.

The villa was surrounded by a huge iron fence. Instead of spikes, there were mammoth tusks. The wrought-iron gate was cast in the shape of musical notes – crotchets and semiquavers.

Bobby and his family paused outside and peered inside curiously.

'We've come to see the brontosaurus,' they said, 'from England.'

'Far out,' said the gatekeeper. 'I'll tell him you're here.' And he picked up the telephone.

After a few minutes he came out, shaking his head.

'I'm sorry, guys. The brontosaurus is in a meeting.'

'But we've come all this way,' complained Bobby. It was like the stage door all over again.

'He started life with us as a birthday cake,' said Bobby's mother.

'Far out,' said the guard. 'I'm sorry. No way I can let you in. Mr Gold is tough – no kidding, guys!'

They looked sadly through the gate.

In the distance they saw the brontosaurus in a swimming costume followed by a procession of butlers with buckets of champagne.

'There he goes,' said the gatekeeper. 'It's time for his mid-day swim.'

'He's got rather fat,' said Bobby's mother disapprovingly.

'We'd better go home,' said his father. 'If we stay here much longer we shall all be ruined. This country is costing me a fortune.'

So they said goodbye to the friendly guard and went back to their hotel. They packed their bags and took the aeroplane back home. Bobby wondered if he would ever see his prehistoric friend again.

At home his friends had lots of questions.

'Is he a superstar?'

'Does he drive a Cadillac?'

'Did you go on his yacht?'

'Does he have a chauffeur?'

'Is he rich and famous?'

Bobby shook his head sadly. 'I don't know,' he said. 'Actually, he wouldn't see us.'

And when he came home in the evening he sat in front of the television and watched the football. The tears ran down his face, and he cried and cried until his mother took him in her arms to comfort him.

'There will be other brontosauruses,' she said.

'But he was my friend.'

33

Bobby had never felt so unhappy in all his life.

The next day he wrote a letter to the brontosaurus. He explained what had happened.

After several weeks the postman brought a reply. The family opened it in great excitement.

'Dear Bobby,' it said. 'The brontosaurus appreciates your kind message. Sincerely, I. Samuel Gold.'

Bobby was sad like he'd never been before.

The holidays ended. He went back to school. The teacher asked the class to write about 'What I did in my holidays'.

Bobby thought hard and then he wrote:

'I lost my best friend.'

The summer was over and the leaves were turning brown. From time to time there were bits of news about the brontosaurus on television. 'He doesn't look very happy,' they said to each other.

Then one day, just before Christmas, the phone rang. 'It's for you,' said his father. 'It sounds like an

American,' he added crossly.

'Hi,' said the voice at the other end. 'It's the *This Is Your Life* studios here. We're doing a New Year spectacular. My producer would like a meeting!'

'Of course,' said Bobby. 'I understand.' And he made the arrangements.

'Now what?' his father demanded as Bobby put the phone down.

'You'll see soon enough,' said Bobby mysteriously. Of course, he had no idea what was going to happen, but he liked to keep his father guessing.

The next day after school the longest car Bobby had ever seen arrived to drive him to the television offices. The producer was very young and wore pink jeans. 'Hi,' he said. 'We want to do a show with the brontosaurus. I've read about you in the newspapers. Something about a birthday cake. Will you come on the programme as a guest?'

'As a guest,' Bobby repeated in a small voice. On

television! 'Sure,' he said, as cool as a cucumber. 'No problem. I've got a few things on, but I expect I can fit it in.'

Then the producer's assistant asked Bobby a lot of questions and he went back home in the long car.

'What have you been doing?' his sister asked.

'Can you keep a secret?'

She nodded.

'The brontosaurus is going to be on *This Is Your Life*.'

'Wowee!!!'

'How will they catch him?' she asked.

'Can you keep another secret?'

Of course she could keep another secret.

'The brontosaurus is coming over for a *première*. They'll catch him then. It won't be difficult. You know how vain he is. He loves television. He'll be over the moon.'

'I can't wait to see him again.'

The day came. An even longer car arrived to take Bobby and his family, in their very best clothes, to the television studios.

The show started.

Yes! There was the brontosaurus looking very surprised. The TV people had flown in all the actors from *Bones!*

I. Samuel Gold was there of course.

The studio was full of prehistoric monsters, pterodactyls, plesiosauruses, dinosaurs and megatheriums.

Everyone was there. Even the wicked Mayor from Bobby's town was there, trying to catch the attention of the camera.

Then the drums began to roll, and there was a smooth voice saying, 'And now ladies and gentlemen, we introduce to you the young man who set the brontosaurus on the road to stardom!'

And on came Bobby and his family.

The audience went wild.

The other guests went bananas.

I. Samuel Gold went white as a ghost.

And the brontosaurus smiled so wide that a little old lady sitting in the front row fainted.

The brontosaurus – who was now incredibly fat – lumbered over to Bobby and nuzzled up against him. Bobby could see there were tears in his eyes.

'I came to see you in America but they wouldn't let me in.'

The brontosaurus looked astonished at this news.

'We flew to Hollywood. Your manager, Mr Gold, turned us away. Are you happy? Tell us, scout's honour?'

The brontosaurus shook his head and looked sad.

Bobby came up close to his scaly friend.
'Welcome home, errant fossil,' he whispered.

Now the show was coming to an end. There was the theme tune, lots of applause and all the guests were given free drinks.

Suddenly there was a crash. Bobby looked up

and saw I. Samuel Gold sailing through the air and landing on his head in a wastepaper basket.

The brontosaurus had just sacked his manager.

There was a commotion as the brontosaurus rushed towards the Exit.

He was pursued by the TV people.

'Let him go,' shouted Bobby. 'He wants to be free!'

In a few minutes the TV people returned. 'He's escaped,' they said. 'What shall we do?'

Bobby said, 'He's happy. He's free. He's where he wants to be. He will return when he wants to.'

'I can't think what got into him,' said the producer.

Bobby did not say anything. But he knew. The brontosaurus was tired of being a superstar.

I. Samuel Gold looked miserable.

But Bobby was smiling.

He knew that the brontosaurus was out there, in the country, by the seaside, among the flowers and the animals.

And of course Bobby knew that one day he would come back to his house in the suburbs and he'd find his old friend sitting in his father's garden, eating his way through the prize roses just like old times.

The Dream Boat Brontosaurus

Dear Boby, i ve gon too
look for a bit of peec
and quite. Perhapps ill
find anuther monster,
pleez dont wurry aboat
mee i ll be bak sun.
   yor frend, B.

So the Brontosaurus was a superstar and *everyone* knew all about him. He was rich, famous and successful. He had all the hamburgers and Coca-Cola he wanted. But there was one big problem.

Nobody would leave him alone.

Every day coachloads of sightseers drove along Bobby's street for a glimpse of the celebrated monster.

'It's like living in a zoo,' complained Bobby's father one day, staring crossly back at a party of Japanese. 'This fossil's nothing but trouble.'

The brontosaurus, who was sitting outside the window eating the flowers as usual, looked offended. 'Don't mind my dad, prehistoric partner,' said Bobby. 'It's just his way of saying he loves you.'

The brontosaurus looked thoughtful.

The next day, when Bobby came down to breakfast, there was no sign of the brontosaurus, just a letter next to his cornflakes. He recognized the palaeolithic handwriting.

'Spelling was never his strong point,' said Bobby's mother.

'I wonder what he's up to?' said Liz, Bobby's sister.

'One dinosaur's more than enough for me,' said his father.

Bobby smiled to himself. He knew that whenever

the brontosaurus disappeared there was always an adventure on the way.

He was right, of course. A few days later, there was a noise in the street. Bobby rushed outside and there was his megalithic companion wearing an amazing sailor suit.

'What's all this about?' asked Bobby, pointing to his clothes.

The brontosaurus gave a wink. Then with a swish of his long scaly tail he planted Bobby on his back and began to run faster . . . faster . . . FASTER . . . *FASTER* . . .

'I didn't know you could fly,' said Bobby.

Suddenly they were at the seaside. The sun was shining. Sea birds danced in the air. And there, in the middle of the bay, was the finest yacht Bobby had ever seen. Painted in huge gold letters on the stern was its name: *Brontosaurus*.

'You always did have a big ego,' said Bobby affectionately.

The brontosaurus gave his friend a look that said: Are you ready for an adventure?

Was he ready? He couldn't wait!

First they met the captain, who was a chimpanzee.

'Haven't I seen you before somewhere?' asked Bobby.

'Och, aye,' replied the captain, a wrinkly old Scot. 'I'm from the zoo. Me and the brontosaurus are old acquaintances.'

'And so are we!' chorused a couple of voices behind him.

Suddenly a couple of smaller chimpanzees in tartan kilts popped up.

'Where did you come from?' asked Bobby with surprise.

'We're the McChimps,' they replied with one voice. 'We used to work at McDonald's. That's how we know the brontosaurus.'

The brontosaurus smiled at the McChimps approvingly.

The *Brontosaurus* was a fabulous sailing boat. There was a saloon with a bar. There was a ballroom with its own orchestra. There was an indoor swimming pool, a private cinema and a helipad. The bedroom was the size of Bobby's house.

'Fan-tastic,' said Bobby.

'What kind of a boat can this be?' Bobby asked, thinking aloud.

'It's a DREAM BOAT,' said the McChimps in unison.

'What's a Dream Boat?' asked Bobby, noticing as he did so that the sea was rushing past at incredible speed, even though the boat appeared to be standing still.

'Look!' said the McChimps, turning him towards the shore.

Bobby looked. The harbour and all the people had gone. For a moment he thought he would panic. Then he saw the reassuring smile of the brontosaurus.

'You never cease to amaze me, antiquated antediluvian,' he said. 'Now what?'

'Make your wish,' said the McChimps. 'Then the Dream Boat will take you on a trip.'

'Where to?'

'You won't know till you close your eyes,' said the McChimps.

Bobby closed his eyes and made an *enormous* wish. He began to feel drowsy and he knew he was drifting off to sleep . . .

When he opened his eyes Bobby was not sure where he was. He thought he could hear the sound of the McChimps having an argument.

He pulled on his clothes and ran up on deck.

The brontosaurus was sitting on a deck-chair holding a map. The McChimps were jumping about, pointing at the shore.

'Hoots, man, we're way off course,' said the McChimps. 'We set the compass wrong. We're supposed to be in the Caribbean.'

'So where are we, actually?' asked Bobby.

'Actually, we're in New York, dumbo,' said the McChimps. 'Don't you know anything?' they groaned. 'Look!'

There behind him was the Statue of Liberty.

'Old scaly-feet likes that lassie,' said the McChimps. 'She makes him feel underweight.'

As they spoke, a motor-boat with a fat customs officer came alongside.

'Where ya from?' he asked. 'And what's ya business?'

'My palaeolithic friend and I,' said Bobby smoothly, 'are studying . . .'

'Cut that out!' said the customs man. 'Where's ya papers?'

The brontosaurus opened his mouth wide in a yawn. The customs man went white. 'No offence, buster. Just doing my dooty.'

'Time for a change of scene,' said the McChimps.

'Shut your eyes, Bobby.'

Bobby shut his eyes. 'Watch that map,' he shouted.

'Count to ten!' cried the McChimps.

Bobby began to count. ONE, TWO, THREE, FOUR, FIVE . . . The wind rushed through his hair. He felt the Dream Boat gathering speed. Perhaps it was flying.

SIX, SEVEN, EIGHT . . . Everything went very still.

NINE, TEN.

'Ten!' said Bobby out loud.

'Open your eyes,' shouted the McChimps.

Bobby opened his eyes and gasped. The Dream Boat was moored next to the greenest tropical island he had ever seen. The sound of steel drums floated across the water.

Bobby put his arms round the brontosaurus, who looked splendid in a pair of Bermuda shorts.

At last, my scaly pal,' he said. 'At last some peace and quiet.'

Bobby and the brontosaurus had the best holiday of their lives. They drank coconut milk and Coca-Cola. The brontosaurus even got a sun-tan. And when he stepped onto the scales he weighed as much as SIXTY policemen.

'Was it like this in the good old days?' Bobby asked. 'I mean before the Ice Age.'

The brontosaurus nodded his head sadly.

'Wouldn't it be terrific if we could leave him behind?' Bobby suggested to the McChimps. 'He hasn't had it so good for centuries!'

'But you don't understand,' they said. 'It's only a dream.'

'Sometimes dreams come true,' Bobby replied. 'Mine did. The brontosaurus started life as a birthday cake. I dreamed he was real. And he was.'

'Och, man, that was in the real world. This is the Dream Boat. Things are always changing on the

Dream Boat. Close your eyes and you'll see!'

The landscape began to shake and rumble. The leaves fell off the trees. The beaches turned white. It became incredibly cold. They were in the Antarctic.

'Who's idea was this?' said Bobby.

'Stay cool, man,' said the McChimps.

The brontosaurus sat in his cabin reading the *Beano*, shivering and drinking hot chocolate. 'You don't like this, do you?' said Bobby. 'And I know why. It reminds you of the Ice Age.'

The brontosaurus nodded. He was beginning to look rather unwell.

'Help!' cried Bobby. 'The brontosaurus won't survive if we stay in this climate.'

The McChimps scratched their heads. 'We're working on it, man. Chill out!'

'Can't you have another dream?' said Bobby.

'We're dreamin', Bobby,' they said. 'We're dreamin'.'

The brontosaurus was already huddled under an enormous duvet. When the McChimps began to snore, Bobby fell asleep as well.

When he woke up it was warmer and the brontosaurus was munching a hamburger in the corner by the ship's compass. He seemed much happier.

Bobby went out on deck. The Dream Boat was moored in a swimming pool inside a huge hall filled with every imaginable kind of craft.

'It's a Boat Show,' said Bobby with surprise.

He leant over the side and shouted to one of the visitors. 'Excuse me,' he said, 'but would you mind telling me where we are just now?'

The man looked astonished. 'This is Australia, mate. And don't you forget it.'

'Whose idea was *this*?' said Bobby turning to the McChimps.

'Not mine,' said the first. 'It's his. He's always wanted to go Down Under. He was talking about it just the other day.'

Now a man in a pair of khaki shorts and a floppy hat appeared on deck.

'G'day, mate,' he said. 'Mind if I step aboard? The name's Bruce. Who's your friend?'

'That's the world-famous brontosaurus. He's come to look at Australia.'

'Fair dinkum,' said Bruce, and began to look about him. 'Nice boat you have here. Does she race?'

Bobby said he didn't know. No one had ever tried.

'What class is she?'

'She's a Dream Boat.'

'Fair dinkum,' said Bruce.

He took Bobby by the arm and pointed round the hall. 'These boats have come from all over the world to race here. Australia's got to win – but we don't have a winner. You say the Dream Boat's a real goer, right?'

The McChimps were excited. 'We'll sail it for you.'

Bruce looked unhappy. 'Aw, give us a break, fellas,' he said. 'If I ship a couple of apes on board – no offence, mind you – I'll be the laughing stock of Australia.'

'No chimps, no Dream Boat,' said Bobby. 'If you lose, you'll be the laughing stock, too.'

Bruce gulped. 'Okay,' he said. He looked at the brontosaurus. 'Will zoo-features want to come along too?'

'Now there's no need to be rude,' said Bobby firmly. 'We're all coming.'

Soon they had the best rooms in the best hotel in Australia, and the brontosaurus had all the kangarooburgers he could possibly want.

The day of the race came. There were yachts from all over the world: France, New Zealand, America, Italy and England.

All the spectators were very excited. The sea was full of sails. The Dream Boat *Brontosaurus* flew the Australian flag. Bruce, Bobby and the brontosaurus

were up bright and early.

It was Bobby who noticed that the McChimps were missing.

'You can't sail without them,' he cried.

Bobby and the brontosaurus rushed off to the hotel. The McChimps were jumping up and down at the window.

'This is dirty work at the crossroads,' said Bobby. 'They're locked in. Now we're done for. Unless . . .'

They rushed back to the Dream Boat just in time for the start of the race. Bruce pretended to be a brilliant navigator, but Bobby and the McChimps knew they had their work cut out. They closed their eyes and made the biggest wish in the world . . . and the Dream Boat swept ahead of all the other yachts in the race.

There were loud cheers as it crossed the line first. BOOM! went the finishing gun.

Bruce was delighted. 'It's a dream come true,' he said proudly.

The sea air had made them all sleepy. Bobby curled up next to the brontosaurus and fell asleep just like that.

When he woke up, he was shivering. The McChimps were leaping about the cabin with bowls of porridge.

The brontosaurus opened an eye and gave his 'Where are we now?' look.

Bobby wiped the steam off the porthole. 'Scotland, of course,' he said. 'No wonder those two are so happy.'

The Dream Boat *Brontosaurus* sailed down the West Coast of Scotland and they all sang 'Over the Sea to Skye'. The McChimps visited all their friends and relations and ate lots of porridge.

One morning, Bobby woke to find the brontosaurus missing.

'He's been out all night,' said the McChimps. They winked. 'He's found a friend.'

There was a strange splashing sound outside. They all went on deck. It was very misty. But they could just make out the shape of the brontosaurus swimming through the water. And at his side was a SECOND dinosaur.

The McChimps were very excited. 'Don't tell us!' they shouted. 'We know who *she* is. She's called Nessie.'

'Welcome aboard, errant fossils,' said Bobby, adding in a whisper, 'She's even more famous than you are.'

The brontosaurus blushed and introduced Nessie. Bobby looked at his watch. 'Time to be on our way,' he said. He wondered what his father would say when he arrived with *two* dinosaurs.

So they tied the Dream Boat *Brontosaurus* up in the harbour and came home to the little house on the edge of the big city.

Everyone was very glad to see them and to hear about all the adventures on the Dream Boat.

'So now he'll be eating my roses again,' said Bobby's father. 'Well, thank goodness there's only one of him.'

'Oh,' said Bobby. 'Did I forget to tell you?'

'What's that? What's that?'

'Er . . . well . . . he's found a friend.'

'He . . . A what, a WHAT!!! A friend!! I don't believe it,' exclaimed his father, jumping out of his chair.

'Well, look for yourself,' said Bobby.

And there in the garden, side by side with Nessie, was the brontosaurus, eating the roses as usual.

'I think this is a dream,' muttered Bobby's father.

'Perhaps it is,' said Bobby cheerfully. 'Wait till you find the chimpanzees in the garage.'

'Time for bed,' said his mother. 'Really, you do tell the tallest stories sometimes, Bobby.'

Bobby smiled. So did the brontosaurus. And so did Nessie.

They knew that this story was true.